NATIONAL
PARKS
of the
U.S.A.

WIDE EYED EDITIONS

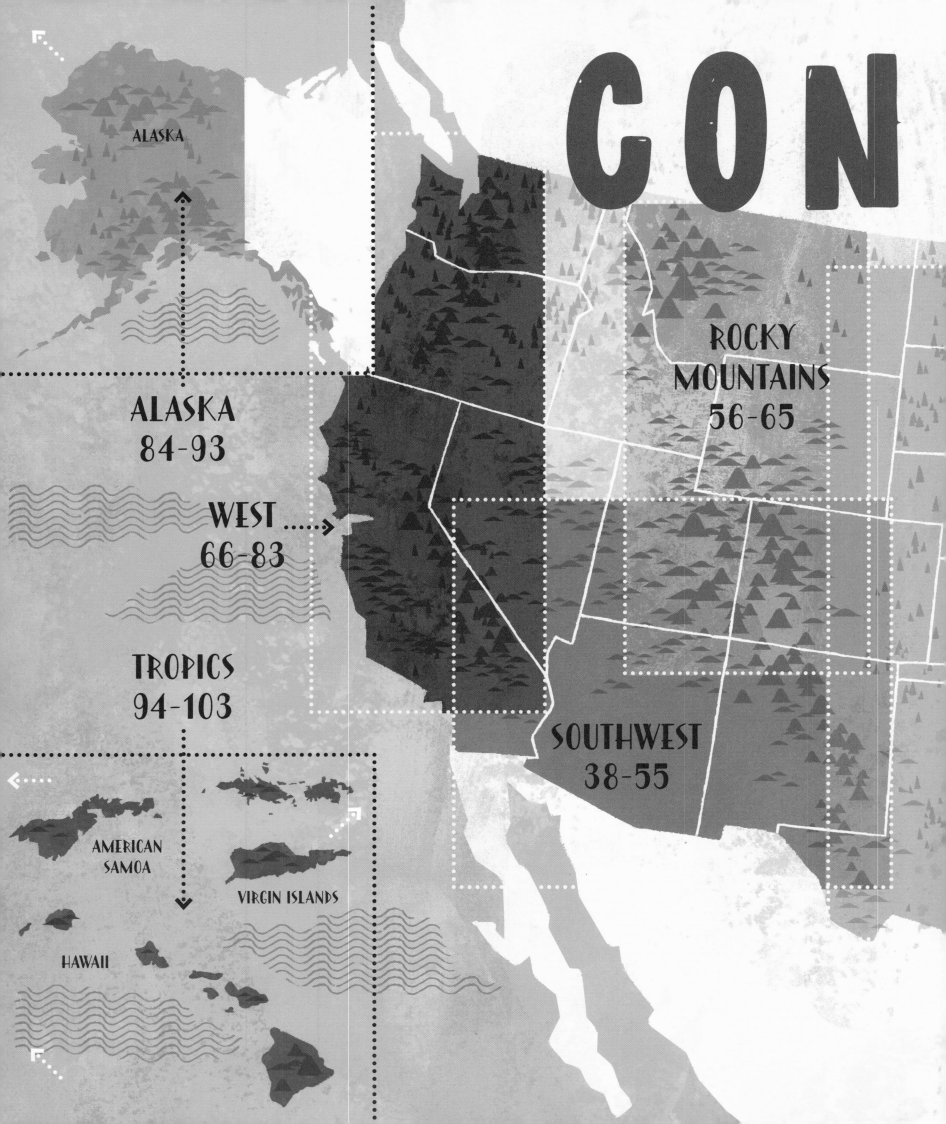

TENTS

CENTRAL
24-37

EAST
6-23

WELCOME TO THE NATIONAL PARKS OF THE U.S.A.

Get ready for a big adventure! On your journey through the national parks, you'll find mind-boggling wonders, from the continent's biggest peak to a mile-deep canyon, dark swamps filled with critters, and volcanoes that pelt lava straight into the sea. Creatures big and small abound in these wild lands, from thundering bison to tiny seahorses. The parks protect some of America's most spectacular landscapes, wild animals, and precious plants.

But these natural reserves didn't always exist. A few forward-thinking citizens dreamed up the idea way back in the 1800s. They saw the flood of pioneers streaming into the American West, gobbling up land for houses, farms, and other human purposes. These visionaries worried that all the majestic vistas would disappear and called for territory to be set aside in its natural state.

In 1872, Congress and President Ulysses S. Grant established the world's first national park, Yellowstone. People came from all over by train and stagecoach to see its unbelievable wonders: geysers shooting hundreds of feet into the sky, hot springs painted wild colors, and huge bears, elk, and wolves!

By the turn of the century, other national parks were born, such as Sequoia, which has trees as big as 20-story buildings, and Yosemite, where waterfalls roar down cliffs taller than skyscrapers. Now the Park Service preserves monuments, battlefields, and other sites, but the 59 national parks are still the cream of the crop. Each one protects a unique landscape and sights that you can't see anywhere else.

What are you waiting for? Turn the page and see what you can discover in the great national parks of the U.S.A.!

EAST

The eastern United States is crowded with big cities, but wild, untamed lands hide in their midst. In the ancient Appalachian Mountains, black bears, deer, and elk roam. Waterfalls trickle and tumble, and mist blankets the valleys like puffy cotton balls. It's a different scene on the coast. In northern waters, lobsters and crabs patrol the seafloor, or hide in tide pools, and loons cry their eerie howls on the surface. In the aquamarine seas of Florida, coral reefs are like bustling, multicolored cities for fish. There are even traffic jams! Because this part of the country was one of the earliest to be settled by Europeans, many of the eastern parks also have historic buildings to explore. Imagine what it was like to be a soldier stationed at a fort 100 years ago, or a settler living off the land in an Appalachian cabin you'd built yourself.

ACADIA

Climb a granite dome for views over the sea or wade into a tide pool to find mussels, limpets, and other creepy crawlies.

SHENANDOAH

In Shenandoah, more than 500 miles of hiking trails wind through leafy forests. Stroll to the top of round mountains or to peaceful waterfalls.

GREAT SMOKY MOUNTAINS

The Smokies were named for the beautiful bluish fog that gathers around their peaks and valleys. Creatures from salamanders to black bears dwell here.

CONGAREE

Paddling a canoe through Cedar Creek, stare up at some of the tallest deciduous trees in America. This is largest old-growth bottomland hardwood forest in the U.S.A.

EVERGLADES

The Everglades are the largest subtropical wilderness in the country. Alligators, panthers, and birds by the thousands live in these humid forests and prairies.

BISCAYNE

Parrotfish, gobies, rays, and sharks are just a few of the animals snorkelers spot in Biscayne Bay, just outside of Miami, Florida's biggest city.

DRY TORTUGAS

With only seven tiny islands, this Florida park is 99% water! Wade in to see corals and tropical fish, then explore Fort Jefferson, one of the country's biggest 19th-century forts.

BISCAYNE

Floating in a boat in Biscayne Bay, you see a huge expanse of turquoise water, islands, and distant mazes of mangrove trees. But 95% of this park is actually underwater! Strap on your snorkel and dip beneath the surface to see a cornucopia of fish and corals, from tiny gobies to colorful parrotfish, who look like they're dressed up for a really tacky dance party. About 600 species of fish live in Biscayne—more than all of the animal species in Yellowstone National Park. There are also plenty of marine mammals like dolphins and manatees. Can you spot a loggerhead turtle? See if you can keep up as she gracefully swims to the surface to take a breath.

BISCAYNE

STATE:
Florida

FOUNDED:
1980

SIZE:
172,974 acres

LOGGERHEAD TURTLE
Sea turtles travel far and wide to find crabs, jellyfish, and seaweed. A female always returns to her birth beach to lay eggs, sometimes a journey of more than 1,000 miles.

BROWN PELICAN
Brown pelicans can store three times as many fish in their beak pouches as they can in their stomachs.

ELKHORN CORAL
This threatened coral lives in shallow water and looks like antlers, sometimes growing bigger than six feet.

FLORIDA STRANGLER FIG
This plant sprouts high on another tree, then spirals its roots down to the ground, often growing so large it shades its host, weakening or killing it.

SCHAUS SWALLOWTAIL
One of the state's rarest butterflies, the Schaus swallowtail lives for only one month and has a neat trick: it can stop midair and suddenly fly backward.

SEAGRASSES
Lush underwater seagrass beds offer food and hiding places for many animals, from tiny shrimp to huge manatees.

ATLANTIC BOTTLENOSE DOLPHIN

These friendly creatures often play in the bow waves of boats. They use echolocation to "see" objects under the water, making clicking sounds and waiting to hear the echoes.

INVASIVE SPECIES: THE LIONFISH

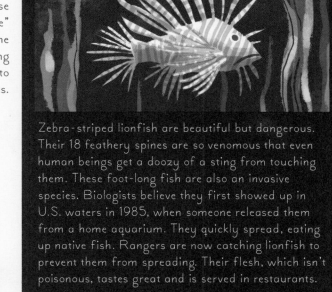

Zebra-striped lionfish are beautiful but dangerous. Their 18 feathery spines are so venomous that even human beings get a doozy of a sting from touching them. These foot-long fish are also an invasive species. Biologists believe they first showed up in U.S. waters in 1985, when someone released them from a home aquarium. They quickly spread, eating up native fish. Rangers are now catching lionfish to prevent them from spreading. Their flesh, which isn't poisonous, tastes great and is served in restaurants.

COCONUT PALM

Palms grow up to 80 feet tall, and their coconuts can float in the ocean for hundreds of miles before sprouting in a new home.

BULL SHARK

Bull sharks eat just about anything, from fish and turtles to birds and even other sharks. They prefer shallow water, sometimes traveling hundreds of miles up rivers.

CORAL REEFS

The oceans are huge, but most sea life lives where there's good food and hiding places, like coral reefs. Corals might look like rocks, but they're actually tiny animals that suck calcium from seawater and create protective limestone skeletons. They grow in all sorts of crazy colors and shapes, creating homes for fish. Like a city, there's activity here day and night. Big fish and eels stop by cleaner stations, where cleaner wrasse, shrimp, and gobies nibble parasites and dead skin off their bodies. Tiny damselfish are farmers and grow algae to eat—but watch out, they are protective and might nip at your mask! And neon-colored parrotfish bite off little pieces of coral and poop it out as sand. Now you know where all that sand around reefs comes from—it's parrotfish poop!

Everglades

The air feels heavy and humid as you paddle through a mangrove forest. Birds squawk and sing overhead, and a manatee glides by. Welcome to the Everglades, the largest subtropical wilderness in the country. In these 1.5 million acres, you'll find diverse habitats, from the open waters of Florida Bay to sawgrass prairies threaded by rivers. While you walk along a boardwalk called the Anhinga Trail, watch for fish circling in the clear water below. A turtle the size of a dinner plate balances on a rock like he's flying, and an alligator floats as still as a log. In the distance, listen for the gators bellowing. It sounds like deep dog growls!

EVERGLADES

STATE:
Florida

FOUNDED:
1947

SIZE:
1,542,526 acres

MANGROVE FORESTS

With the help of their stilt-like roots, red, white, and black mangrove trees grow over shallow water. They form mazelike thickets that protect the coast from storms and are tough for humans to travel through. But birds and fish don't mind! Pelicans, wood storks, and cormorants nest in mangrove branches. Sharks, grouper, and snapper all raise babies here. You might even see tree crabs clambering upside down on branches. If you startle them, they'll drop down into the water—or your canoe!

CLAMSHELL ORCHID
Flower poachers have stolen so many of these plants, there aren't many left. See if you can spot one of their rare, spectacular blooms.

LIGUUS TREE SNAIL
Tree snails come in wild colors and stripes—green, pink, yellow, orange, and brown. They slide along tree branches on trails of their own mucus.

CARDINAL AIRPLANT
Airplants survive by attaching to a tree and sucking nutrients out of the air and rain. Frogs like to lay eggs in their leaves.

BALD CYPRESS TREE
Cypress trees grow in groups in mucky areas, creating leafy domes, like green churches that make shady homes for frogs, birds, and other creatures.

SAWGRASS
Sawgrass grows at least as tall as you in great waving meadows, but be careful—they have rows of tiny, sharp teeth.

SPOONBILL
Roseate spoonbills nest in big, noisy groups in mangrove trees. During mating, a couple "kisses" by crossing their long, spoon-shaped bills.

WEST INDIAN MANATEE
Gentle, slow-moving manatees, or "sea cows," are mammals just like us, but they live their whole lives underwater, growing as big as 1,500 pounds just on a diet of marine plants.

ALLIGATOR
Alligators were once endangered because humans hunted them for their belly skin, which makes nice leather. Now they thrive in southern Florida, growing up to 15 feet long.

FLORIDA PANTHER
You need patience and good luck to spot these rare, secretive cats. They silently stalk the Everglades for deer, hogs, raccoons, and rabbits.

MARSH RABBIT
Unlike their landlubbing cousins, these bunnies love to swim. They paddle through swamps searching for herbs, flowers, and other plants to nibble on.

HUMAN THREAT: THE PLUME TRADE

There were once so many birds in the Everglades that great flocks blotted out the sun. But in the late 1800s and early 1900s, fashionable ladies started to wear fancy hats decorated with bird feathers. The style encouraged hunters to kill beautiful birds by the millions, devastating the Everglades. Bird lovers responded by founding some of the country's first conservation clubs, which helped pass laws to protect these feathery friends. Now you can see birds like herons and snowy egrets all over the Everglades.

GREAT SMOKY
MOUNTAINS

More than 10 million people visit Great Smoky Mountains National Park every year—more than any other park in the country. Why is it so popular? Find out by hiking through five different forest types, from low, dry hardwoods to high spruce woods that smell like Christmas trees. Scenic vistas over the mountains pop out everywhere. In spring, the land is covered in wildflowers. In fall, the deciduous trees turn into a rainbow of reds, oranges, and golds. Hear some sticks crackling? It could be one of park's 1,500 black bears poking around for berries or maybe a white-tailed deer looking for forage. Rain is common, so cinch up your rain slicker—or just enjoy the wet, cool mist and the sounds of moving water that ring through the forest.

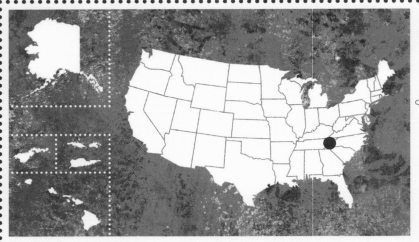

GREAT SMOKY MOUNTAINS

STATE:
North Carolina
& Tennessee

FOUNDED:
1934

SIZE:
522,427 acres

DOWNY WOODPECKER
Rat-tat-tat-tat-tat-tat! That's the rapid-fire sound of a downy woodpecker hammering its hard beak against a tree in the forest.

BLACK BEAR
Black bears eat mainly nuts, fruit, dead animals and the occasional ant colony. They can run as fast as 30 miles per hour.

BROOK TROUT
These colorful striped fish live in cool streams high in the mountains. Fishers love them for their beauty and delicate flavor.

JACK-IN-THE-PULPIT
This park has more flowering plants than any other park—over 1,500 species. Jack-in-the-pulpit's roots are toxic when raw, but Native Americans knew to dry them and cook them before eating.

PYGMY SHREW
This tiny burrowing mammal weighs less than a dime but can give birth to as many as eight babies at a time.

SYNCHRONOUS FIREFLIES
Fireflies, also known as "lightning bugs," only live for about three weeks, but during their brief lives, they put on amazing light shows with their glowing bellies. Synchronous fireflies, one of the park's 19 species of lightning bugs, are the only kind that can time their flashes all at once. In May and June, these colorful beetles light up whole hillsides in waves of greenish-yellow lights and attract visitors on firefly tours.

FLAME AZALEA

Growing as high as 12 feet, which is twice as tall as a grown man, flame azaleas have showy reddish orange flowers the size of golf balls.

SALAMANDERS

Thirty species of salamanders live in this park, more than any other place in the world. Pick them up with a plastic bag so you don't damage their skin, which they use to breathe.

GREAT HORNED OWL

With excellent hearing and night vision, the great horned owl swoops down after dark to grab mice, snakes, rabbits, and even other owls.

EASTERN HEMLOCK

Some of the park's eastern hemlocks sprouted as long ago as the 1750s. That's before our country was born!

WATERFALLS

More than 2,000 miles of streams weave through Great Smoky Mountains National Park. With lots of steep land, that means only one thing: waterfalls! Ramsey Cascades is the tallest waterfall in the park, tumbling down slippery algae-covered rocks for about 100 feet. Sometimes, if the sun angle is just right, you can see tiny rainbows in the waterfalls' mist.

CEMETERIES

Euro-American settlers lived in the hidden valleys of the Smokies starting in the early 1800s. Since they were so far from towns, everything had to be made by hand from materials found in the forest, so they were often skilled woodworkers and craftspeople. With no doctors, schools, or stores, life was tough. You can still visit their old barns and cabins today, and about 150 cemeteries remain. Find the old headstones overgrown with grass and shrubs. Some date back more than 200 years.

Acadia

Lace up your hiking boots! This park is known for steep trails that beeline straight up granite mountains. Some paths are so steep they have iron ladders and rungs. You could be the first person in the country to see the sunrise if you get to the top of Cadillac Mountain before dawn. Far below, seals and porpoises play in the cold deep-blue water, and lobsters and crabs crawl about on the seafloor. Paddle a kayak through the silky waters and take a whiff of the briny air. You might spot an eagle swooping overhead. Hear that long, spooky wail? That's the cry of a loon traveling through the fog.

ACADIA

STATE:
Maine

FOUNDED:
1916

SIZE:
49,630 acres

PEREGRINE FALCON

Falcons dive as fast as 200 miles per hour, striking other birds in midair, and then eating them.

WARBLER

These small colorful birds love Acadia because it has diverse forests and wetlands full of delicious insects. Listen for their complex songs, pips, and cheeps.

WHITE-TAILED DEER

White-tailed deer live everywhere from the Arctic to Peru. They escape predators by hiding, running quickly, and moving silently.

SUGAR MAPLE

Sugar maples turn red, orange, and gold every autumn. In spring, they release sugary sap, which locals have made into maple syrup for centuries.

COMMON JUNIPER

This tough shrub grows spiny needles that repel hungry animals, and survives wind and cold by tucking behind rocks.

WETLANDS

Unlike tidal mudflats, which smell like rotten eggs, wetlands smell fresh and earthy. If the three-foot grasses are taller than you, stand up on a log to look around. Warblers and ducks fill the air with songs, trills, and quacks. Frogs croak, while dragonflies zoom around looking for insects to eat. In the distance, a beaver contemplates the next tree he'll bite. Sphagnum moss lives in some wetlands. This soft plant has antiseptic properties and was used for bandages during the Civil War.

BLUEBERRY

Pluck these sweet deep-blue berries from sunny mountaintops, meadows, and forest edges for a tasty snack.

FERNS

Under the cool, moist shade of forests you'll find a sea of green ferns, some with fronds as big as 2.5 feet.

TIDE POOLS

Roll up your pants and wade into a tide pool to look for some of the creatures the sea leaves behind. Catch a rock, spider, or green crab as it skitters about. Nearby, an amphipod scurries on its many feet to hide under seaweed. In another pool, find treasures like periwinkles, mussels, and sea slugs. Pick up a sea star, turn it over, and you might spot a jellylike blob. That's the star's stomach. It oozes out to digest food, then sucks back into its body! Around and above you, seagulls squawk and flap about. Look out—they drop mussels and sea urchins on the rocks to break them open for food.

LOBSTER

Lobsters are ill-tempered beasts, eating just about anything that crosses their paths and fighting to determine who's boss. They also molt their shells and grow new ones as many as 25 times during the first five years of life. No wonder they're grumpy.

PORPOISE

Pfffff! That's the sound of a porpoise exhaling through its blowhole. These relatives of the dolphins live close to shore in shallow waters, but they're very shy.

AMERICAN MINK

Minks are the size of small house cats. They hunt fish, frogs, and mice and are prized for their warm, luxurious fur.

Some people call the middle of America flyover country because so many planes sail over it. But get your boots on the ground and you'll be rewarded with unique sights and big open landscapes from the Great Lakes to the Great Plains. Mysterious rocky hoodoos rise out of the badlands, and caves snake deep into the earth. Mountains soar out of the desert like dinosaur teeth, and majestic rivers gouge out canyons. From north to south, the climate varies from frigid to sweltering, which means there's a fantastic array of animals. Bison herds still graze the plains. Flocks of sandhill cranes and other migratory birds fly overhead. And lizards, scorpions, and javelinas dart about the deserts.

THEODORE ROOSEVELT

Teddy Roosevelt visited these plains to hunt bison and test his manhood in his 20s. The landscape inspired him so much that after he became president, he protected more than 230 million acres of public land.

WIND CAVE

Because of different atmospheric pressures between this cave and the earth's surface, strong winds barrel through the entrance, blowing your hat off your head.

BIG BEND

In this remote West Texas park, coyotes, mountain lions, and rattlesnakes ramble the desert under night skies so dark the Milky Way looks like a glowing white ribbon.

CENTRAL

VOYAGEURS

Hop in a canoe, kayak, or motorboat to see this maze of lakes and boreal forests. Keep an ear out for the munching of a moose or the howls of a wolf pack.

ISLE ROYALE

This 45-mile island in the middle of Lake Superior is home to wolves, moose, thick forests, and swamps that smell like muck and flowers.

CUYAHOGA VALLEY

Nineteenth-century buildings and even a covered bridge remain in this historic park, which protects a serene river valley, wetlands full of birds and beavers, and Ohio's tallest waterfall.

BADLANDS

Saber-toothed cats, three-toed horses, and camels all lived in this region millions of years ago. Now there are so many fossils, visitors just about trip over them.

MAMMOTH CAVE

Spelunkers have mapped more than 400 miles of passageways in Mammoth Cave, the longest cavern system in the world. Some sections are no wider than a basketball.

HOT SPRINGS

How does a hot, steamy, all-natural bath sound? People have flocked to these mineral springs for centuries, and still do!

BADLANDS

The Lakota people gave the Badlands a fearsome name because of their crumbly stone, vicious winds, and lack of water. Now people come from all over to see bizarre striped pinnacles and some of the world's richest fossil beds, which protect the remains of ancient creatures. Paleontologists have dug around since the 1840s, but they are still discovering new specimens today. In 2010, a seven-year-old girl found a rare saber-toothed cat fossil with bite marks on it from a fight millions of years ago! What might you find? Despite the high winds and prairie fires, animals like bison, coyotes, hawks, prairie dogs, and pronghorn live here. The landscape continues to change as rain and wind scour off layers of rock. Rangers say you only have about 500,000 years to visit before these jagged hills and spires wash away.

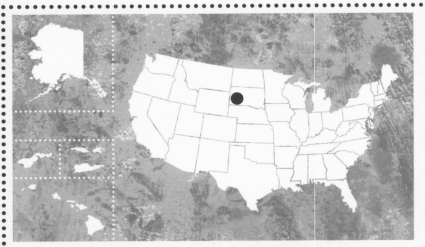

BADLANDS

STATE:
South Dakota

FOUNDED:
1939

SIZE:
242,756 acres

TWO-TAILED SWALLOWTAIL
One of the larger butterflies in the West, this insect makes a protective tent out of leaves while it feeds.

PRONGHORN
Pronghorn antelope are the continent's fastest land mammals. They can sprint up to 60 miles per hour to escape predators like bobcats and coyotes.

RATTLESNAKE
To find prey, prairie rattlesnakes use their keen night vision, heat-detecting organs, and forked tongues, which can "smell." Hollow fangs inject venom before they eat their prey whole.

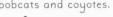

PLAINS COTTONWOOD
Not many trees survive on the prairie with so little water, lots of fire, and plant-eating animals. But the plains cottonwood survives by living near streams and growing super fast.

• MIXED PRAIRIES

Badlands National Park has one of the largest swaths of mixed-grass prairie left in the country. Some of the grasses grow higher than an adult's waist. It can look like just a sea of waving grass but this is tasty and nutritious food for animals like pronghorn, bison, and prairie dogs. These native plants also keep the soil in place so it doesn't blow away and create dust storms.

BURROWING OWL

Only a little bigger than a robin, this small owl hangs out underground in prairie-dog burrows and eats lots of insects—even scorpions.

PRAIRIE DOG

Prairie dogs are social and dig burrows with lots of rooms to hide from attackers. They recognize members of their town with a secret sniff or "kiss."

FOSSILS

Between 26 and 34 million years ago, rhinoceroses, five-foot-tall piglike creatures, and alligators roamed a swampy tropical forest. Now paleontologists find fossils of all sorts of extinct critters, including three-toed horses, camels, and the first dogs and cats. Even older fossil beds host fantastic finds from a time when the area was a vast inland sea, about 67 to 75 million years ago. Imagine sea turtles the size of cars and reptiles like the mosasaur, a giant toothy sea lizard that grew to 60 feet long.

BISON

Weighing as much as a small car, bison (also known as buffalo) are the largest land mammals in North America.

TUFTED EVENING PRIMROSE

This white flower stays open all night, attracting nocturnal insects with long tongues, such as the giant hawk moth.

BIG BEND

The air is dry and the sun is hot in the Chihuahuan Desert, but this park is full of life. About 60 species of cacti and 400 bird species carve out a living here. Watch for cottontails and jackrabbits zigzagging through thorny plants. In the middle of the park, mountain lions and black bears roam a small kingdom of spiky peaks. See those furry piglike animals with pointy snouts? Those are javelinas foraging for plants. What gives this desert so much life is the Rio Grande, which marks the border with Mexico and sculpts canyons like Santa Elena, where you can crane your neck to see cliffs higher than New York's Empire State Building. When evening comes, take in the clear night sky and listen for the howls of coyotes.

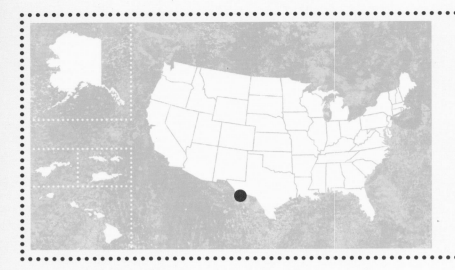

BIG BEND

STATE:
Texas

FOUNDED:
1944

SIZE:
801,116 acres

LUCIFER HUMMINGBIRD

Lucifer hummingbirds collect plants, flowers, and even old spiderwebs to make their nests, which are often perched high up in a cactus.

PRICKLY PEAR CACTUS

During wet years, the biggest prickly pear cacti grow delicious red fruits that are as sweet as apples.

MOUNTAIN LION

Mountain lions can eat as much as 30 pounds of food in one sitting. Visitors report about 150 sightings of these big cats in the park per year.

HOT SPRINGS

Don't forget your swimsuit. Groundwater heated deep in the earth bubbles out of the desert on the north bank of the Rio Grande at 105 degrees— that's as hot as bathwater! The ruins of a former resort with an historic bathhouse built in 1909 still collects the water in a big steamy pool. Slip in for a soak in the ancient waters, as they are believed to have therapeutic effects!

JAVELINA

Javelinas (pronounced havelinas) live in herds and survive with very little water by eating the juicy pads of prickly pear cacti.

BLUEBONNETS

In spring, the desert explodes in colorful wildflowers and cactus blooms. Bluebonnets grow up to four feet tall and are so abundant they turn roadsides blue.

SKY ISLANDS

About 15,000 years ago, the last ice age was wrapping up and forests still covered the area. As the climate warmed, trees sprouted on higher and cooler ground. Eventually, the whole area turned into a desert and the forests survived only in cool "sky islands" like the Chisos Mountains, which rise to 8,000 feet. Now these shady hideouts are home to rare plant species found nowhere else on earth. One grass, the Guadalupe fescue, is so rare, fewer than 200 tufts survive high up in the mountains.

CENTURY PLANT

The largest agave in the park, the century plant grows between 20 and 50 years before blooming one precious time, and then it dies.

BLACK-TAILED JACKRABBIT

These hares can hop 20 feet when panicked. They have up to six litters of as many as eight babies annually.

SPADEFOOT TOAD

To hold in moisture, spadefoot toads hang out underground in a coat of slime. When they hear rain, they quickly find a puddle, sing to find other toads, and mate. Tadpoles hatch and grow up in two weeks!

ROADRUNNER

Roadrunners rarely fly but they can run about 15 miles per hour. When food is scarce, females occasionally feed younger hatchlings to their older siblings!

SOTOL

Native Americans ate the seeds and flower stalks of sotol. They also used parts of the plant to make baskets, roofs, and walking sticks.

33

ISLE ROYALE

To get to this wild 45-mile-long island, take a boat or seaplane across Lake Superior, one of the biggest freshwater lakes in the world. Get ready to hike because there are no roads or cars. Tromp through boreal forests to find blueberries, raspberries, strawberries, and thimbleberries that you can pluck right from the bushes. Not many animals make the long swim, so you won't see skunks, raccoons, or bears. But you might spot a moose browsing in a lake or hear a red squirrel chattering in the trees. After dark, light up your campfire, but don't leave anything lying around. Mischievous foxes often steal campers' belongings and hide them in the woods!

ISLE ROYALE

STATE:
Michigan

FOUNDED:
1940

SIZE:
571,802 acres

LICHENS

More than 600 species of lichen live here. They can appear as tiny hard webs on the ground, light green beards hanging from trees, or splotches of orange paint on rocks.

SWAMP FORESTS

As you walk along wooden boards over a bog, bumblebees and mosquitoes buzz around you. Mosses and sedges crowd the mucky soil. Bend down to look inside a pitcher plant, which eats insects. Bugs get trapped inside, and the plant's digestive juices turn them into insect soup! If you're lucky, you'll see a moose ambling through, eating up to 40 pounds of greenery each day. Catch that whiff? That raspberry vanilla fragrance comes from rose begonias.

THIMBLEBERRY

Pucker up! Tons of these tart red berries grow on Isle Royale. Larger than raspberries, they fit on top of your fingers like thimbles.

LOON

With their powerful legs, loons take deep dives to catch fish. Their red eyes help them see well underwater.

MOSSES

These soft green plants carpet the forests and rocks of Isle Royale. They even grow on moose poop!

SHIPWRECKS

Lake Superior has fierce storms and rugged coastline, including sharp rocks that lie just below the surface. Over the years, many ships have met their doom on these shores. Preserved by the cold water, more than 40 shipwrecks still lie right where they sank. Scuba divers drop beneath the surface to swim through spooky old hallways, cabins, and engine rooms.

GRAY WOLF AND MOOSE

Moose first arrived on the island in the early 1900s, but no one knows how they got here. Did they swim or did someone bring them? Wolves arrived in the 1940s by walking across the frozen lake from Canada. Since then, the populations of the two animals have risen and fallen in a dance. Wolves hunt moose for food and thin the population of sick or injured animals. But when there aren't very many moose, wolves decline. Scientists have been studying the relationship between these species since 1958, the longest study on predators and prey in the world.

COMMON GARTER SNAKE

The garter snakes that live on Isle Royale are usually black with creamy stripes but some have rare designs like orangey red spots and stripes.

PASSAGE ISLAND LIGHTHOUSE

Without the powerful lamps and foghorns of historic lighthouses, more ships might have crashed on the shores of Lake Superior. Passage Island Lighthouse is the northernmost American light in the Great Lakes and was switched on in 1882. But even this sturdy stone house, built about 60 feet above lake level, wasn't immune to winter's fury. One ferocious storm in 1905 caused waves so high, they broke the kitchen windows and flooded the house!

LAKE TROUT

In the waters surrounding Isle Royale, fishermen have caught lake trout that weigh 45 pounds—as big as a medium-sized dog!

FRESHWATER MUSSELS

Chickenbone Lake is home to six million freshwater mussels. Some mussels in the park grow as big as dinner plates.

CAPITOL REEF

Hike among enormous stone domes and arches, eat fruit from 100-year-old Mormon orchards and check out ancient rock art made by indigenous people.

BRYCE CANYON

Hundreds of red, pink, orange, and white stone statues crowd Bryce's slopes like a colorful frozen forest.

ARCHES

More than 2,000 red stone arches dot this rocky land. You can also see cliffs that look like Swiss cheese, as well as delicate pinnacles.

GREAT BASIN

Climb a 13,000-foot peak, crawl though caves, and marvel at bristlecone pines—the oldest trees in the world.

ZION

In a slot canyon the width of your living room, gaze up at sandstone cliffs 1,000 feet high, like the walls of a natural cathedral.

DEATH VALLEY

The largest national park in the continental U.S., Death Valley is outrageously hot, with temperatures that top 120 degrees in summer.

PETRIFIED FOREST

Through a process of petrification, 200-million-year-old logs buried in a riverbed slowly turned to stone. Now they form beautiful rainbow-colored petrified wood.

GRAND CANYON

A mile deep and 18 miles wide, the Grand Canyon has rock layers that are as old as two billion years.

JOSHUA TREE

Bizarre Joshua trees, with lots of fuzzy-looking arms, sprout out of the Mojave Desert as far as the eye can see.

SAGUARO

Saguaros are the biggest cacti in the world, weighing up to six tons—about as much as a pickup truck!

CANYONLANDS

Sandstone stretches in every direction in all sorts of imaginative shapes—tables, bridges, statues, and needles.

MESA VERDE

This green mesa protects the magnificent stone palaces of the Ancestral Puebloan people, who lived here between 700 and 1,400 years ago.

CARLSBAD CAVERNS

More than 100 limestone caverns wend below the earth's surface. Every evening, thousands of bats fly out of the caves for their evening meal.

GUADALUPE MOUNTAINS

About 260 to 270 million years ago, a huge sea covered this land. Now an enormous fossilized reef remains, along with fossils of extinct sea creatures.

Many of the Southwest parks were founded for their bizarre geology—in other words, crazy-looking rocks! Stone arches and skinny pinnacles stretch into the blue desert sky, higher than three-story buildings. The nation's largest canyon plummets more than a mile deep into the earth, and colorful, sparkly, petrified logs litter an old riverbed. These otherworldly lands can seem devoid of life, but lots of plants and animals find homes here. Sagebrush scents the air, and prickly pear and cholla cacti bloom in colors as bright as stoplights. Lizards sun themselves in the heat of noontime, and coyotes and mountain lions prowl the night. Long before us, the ancients knew about the beauty of such landscapes, too. Discover the corncobs, stone pots, and magnificent cliff palaces they left behind long ago.

Grand Canyon

Floating on a rubber raft down the Colorado River, you hear a distant rumble. It grows louder and louder. Hold on tight, that's the sound of a whitewater rapid! Some of these waves are bigger than a small house. This powerful water makes a great roller-coaster ride. It's also the force that carved the Grand Canyon, the biggest chasm in the country at 18 miles wide and more than 5,000 feet deep. You'll see many wonders on your 277-mile journey through it. A bright turquoise stream tumbles into the river. Bighorn sheep tiptoe across cliffs. Rare condors swoop above, and cacti bloom in colors as vibrant as crayons. Look carefully and you might spot the stacked rocks and square windows of a house built centuries ago by Native Americans.

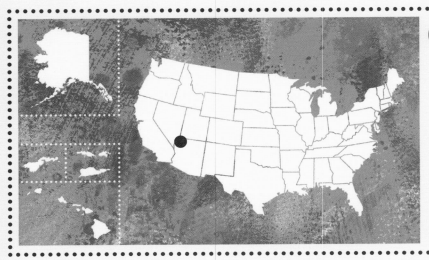

GRAND CANYON

STATE:
Arizona

FOUNDED:
1919

SIZE:
1,217,403 acres

LITTLE BROWN BAT

Bats are the only mammals that can fly. There are 22 bat species in the canyon, which has plenty of caves, cliffs, and old mines where they roost during the day.

RINGTAIL

Like circus performers, ringtails climb straight up and down cliffs, squeeze into tight spaces, turn their hind legs 180 degrees, and even do cartwheels!

CALIFORNIA CONDOR

One of the rarest birds in the U.S., the California condor is a scavenger and soars on an almost 10-foot wingspan looking for dead animals to feast on.

CLARET CUP HEDGEHOG CACTUS

In spring, claret cup cacti erupt in dozens of lipstick-red blooms pollinated by hummingbirds.

SPRINGS AND SEEPS

The canyon is very dry, but water travels deep underground. If you see an explosion of green plants on a cliff, you know you've found one of the 600-plus springs where water comes to the surface. These are often special quiet places known only to wildlife and intrepid adventurers. Listen to the *drip drip* of water and the song of a canyon wren. Breathe in the fresh scents of maidenhair ferns and scarlet monkeyflower. Stay still and you might spot birds taking a drink, shy frogs swimming about, or newly hatched tadpoles.

• INVASIVE SPECIES: TAMARISK

In the 19th century, Americans planted tamarisk to control erosion. Little did they know that this Eurasian plant would grow gangbusters. It spread to rivers and streams throughout the West, slurping up precious water and growing so fast it edged out native plants. Now crews in the Grand Canyon uproot or kill tamarisk with pesticides in order to allow native plants room to grow.

MORMON TEA

Native Americans used to brew an energizing tea from this plant's stems and create tattoos from its charcoal.

RABBITBRUSH

Bright yellow rabbitbrush is a very useful plant. Deer and hares eat it, and birds and rodents nest under it. Native Americans once used it to make yellow dye, cold medicine, and chewing gum.

BIGHORN SHEEP

Desert bighorn sheep clamber up and down rock faces that would make human beings shudder. The steep terrain is their hideout from predators like mountain lions.

CAVES

Scientists estimate that there are about 1,000 caves hidden in the Grand Canyon, but fewer than half of them have been explored. Already spelunkers have discovered amazing treasures in these stone tunnels, like the mummified remains of extinct ice age animals and twig figurines left by ancient indigenous people. What wild mysteries might still hide in these dark chambers?

BARK SCORPION

The most venomous scorpions on the continent, these thumb-size insects grab smaller bugs with their pincers and sting them with their tails. A mama scorpion can carry up to 30 babies on her back.

DEATH VALLEY

Can you imagine what 134 degrees feels like? That record-high temperature was recorded in the shade in 1913 in Death Valley, making it the hottest place on Earth. Death Valley is also the driest and lowest place in North America, but don't let its alarming name scare you. It's full of wonders—and besides, animals don't seem to mind the harsh conditions. Bighorn sheep, cottontails, reptiles, and even tiny fish all make homes here, but they're tough to spot. Inspect smooth sand dunes in the morning to see the tracks of kangaroo rats, lizards, and rattlesnakes, then careen down on a sled! Don't miss crunching along the crusty surface of Badwater Basin, which is the lowest point in America at 282 feet below sea level. Its surface is made of the same kind of salt you find on your dinner table!

DEATH VALLEY

STATE:
California and Nevada

FOUNDED:
1994

SIZE:
3,340,370 acres

PINACATE BEETLE

Also known as a stinkbug, the pinacate beetle stands on its head when threatened. Don't pick it up or it'll spray a smelly black liquid on you!

DESERT TORTOISE

Desert tortoises spend up to nine months of the year hibernating underground, only emerging in spring and fall when the weather is nice. They can live more than 50 years.

DEVILS HOLE PUPFISH

This thumb-size iridescent blue swimmer is one of the rarest fish in the world, living only in Devils Hole, a watery cavern in Death Valley.

KIT FOX

To escape the heat, kit foxes hide in underground dens during the day and then come out in the cool of the night to hunt kangaroo rats, bunnies, reptiles, and insects.

PICKLEWEED

The humble pickleweed has a secret that helps it survive in Death Valley's salt flats and marshes: It can stand an incredible amount of salt. Smash it and it smells like the ocean—even a little fishy!

FLASH FLOODS

Desert soil is pretty hard and doesn't absorb water very well. When intense storms come, water moves fast over the land and collects quickly in low places like canyons. Even if a storm is miles away, the water can rise quickly and powerfully, sweeping away boulders, logs, animals, and even big dumpsters! These floods are what have shaped the canyons and buttes over many years.

PHENOMENON: MOVING ROCKS

Deep in Death Valley, there is an old dry lakebed, a playa, 1,000 feet deep with hardened mud. Rocks as heavy as 700 pounds sit there with long trails behind them in the mud. For years, people were mystified. It looked as if the rocks had moved by themselves! In 2011, scientists happened to be there when the rocks moved. The valley fills with water and freezes into thin panes of ice. On a sunny day, the wind pushes the ice over a cushion of water–driving the rocks too, which leaves trails in the mud. Mystery solved!

RED-TAILED HAWK
You can identify a red-tailed hawk–the most common hawk on the continent–by its telltale crimson tail and its high-pitched scream.

SUPER BLOOMS
Death Valley is very hot and dry, not exactly perfect conditions for flowers to grow. But about every 10 years, freakish rains come and wildflowers that were dormant grow like crazy, creating a colorful carpet. See if you can spot the prized desert five-spot.

KANGAROO RAT
Kangaroo rats suck moisture from seeds, which they carry in cheek pouches and store in burrows. To bathe, they roll around in the dust.

CHUCKWALLA
These large lizards don't need to drink at all, which is lucky as Death Valley has an average annual rainfall of 2.36 inches. Chuckwallas get liquid from the insects and plants they eat.

JOSHUA TREE
The wild, twisty Joshua tree isn't a tree or a cactus, but a yucca plant that can grow 30 feet tall. It relies on one single moth, the yucca moth, to pollinate it.

47

BRYCE
CANYON

On a big slope shaped like a theater, hundreds of skinny rock formations stand like a frozen audience. These wild skinny stones are called "hoodoos," formed by wind and rain eroding the rocks over time. They can be taller than 10-story buildings. Bryce Canyon has more of them than any other place in the world. Walk through towers naturally decorated with all sorts of colors—red, pink, orange, beige, and white. Their hues seem to change with the angle of the sun. But this park isn't just about rocks. There are lots of living things here too, from stealthy mountain lions that patrol remote areas of the park to the tiniest pink wildflower that clings to life in the sandy soil.

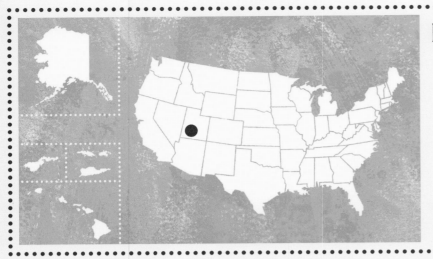

BRYCE CANYON

STATE:
Utah

FOUNDED:
1928

SIZE:
35,835 acres

VIOLET-GREEN SWALLOW
Like acrobats, these colorful swallows dart and dive through the air with their mouths open wide to catch insects.

• STARRY NIGHT SKIES

Because it's in the desert, Bryce Canyon doesn't see a whole lot of clouds all year round. It's also miles from any cities, so it is extremely dark at night. That means that without any "light pollution" the night sky is awash with stars that are invisible to city dwellers. Look up and you'll see a huge murky-white band across the dome of the heavens. That's the Milky Way, our galaxy full of countless stars, the same glowing stripe that American Indians looked up at hundreds of years ago.

COYOTE
Hear those eerie barks and howls after dark? Those are coyotes calling to gather up the members of their pack.

RAVEN
Ravens are incredibly smart. Using teamwork, they can break into locked trash cans and unzip backpacks. Some biologists believe they communicate with a basic language.

TARANTULA HAWK
This giant wasp is rumored to have the worst sting on the planet, but not to worry, it's not interested in you. A female tarantula hawk stings a tarantula to paralyze it, and then lays an egg in its belly. When the egg hatches, the grub eats the tarantula's organs before flying away.

COTTONTAIL RABBIT
Just about every predator, from mountain lions to coyotes, likes to eat little cottontails. Good thing they reproduce quickly. They can have babies as early as three months of age.

LIGHTNING STORMS

You feel the wind pick up, the sky darkens with ominous clouds, and all of the sudden the birds hush. BOOM! Thunder rolls through the sky. A storm is within ten miles, which means it's time to find cover. Find a car or a building and avoid trees or tall objects that are isolated in the desert—lightning likes to hit high points. But just as quickly as these summer monsoons sweep through, the sky clears and the sun emerges again, sometimes within minutes.

BRYCE CANYON PAINTBRUSH
This magenta flower makes food through photosynthesis, but also feeds on other plants by sucking nutrients out of their roots.

SHORT-HORNED LIZARD
When under attack, this spiny reptile can puff up to twice its size, change colors, and even shoot blood through its eyes!

DOUGLAS FIR
Native Americans made a skin salve from this tree's pitch and a dye from its bark. Some even burned its cones to halt the rain.

BRISTLECONE PINE
These gnarly twisted pine trees are some of the longest-lived beings on earth. The oldest known bristlecone was 4,900 years old.

ARROWHEADS AND POTSHERDS

Between about 200 and 1200, Fremont and Anasazi people roamed these areas, and from 1200 the Paiute Indians lived here. They believed that the fortress of hoodoos were once ancient people, who had lived here but were frozen into stone as a punishment for their bad deeds. The Paiute's arrowheads and potsherds still hide among the rocks.

MESA VERDE

About 1,400 years ago, on a forested mesa, a group of early people built pithouses and extravagant palaces high up in alcoves on cliff faces. They etched footholds in the vertical rock so they could clamber up and down; farmed beans, corn, and squash; and gathered seeds and fruit. The Ancestral Pueblo people, once known as the Anasazi, left around 700 years ago but about 600 cliff dwellings remain right where they were left, preserved by the dry climate. In 1906 Mesa Verde became the first national park founded to protect archaeology. Wander through spooky stone rooms, keep a lookout for potsherds and half-eaten corncobs, and scan the cliffs for petroglyphs and charcoal marks from fires that blew out centuries ago.

MESA VERDE

STATE:
Colorado

FOUNDED:
1906

SIZE:
52,074 acres

CHAPIN MESA MILKVETCH

A very rare plant, the Chapin Mesa milkvetch only lives on Mesa Verde and nearby tribal lands. In late spring, a single plant can erupt into more than 50 white flowers.

COLLARED LIZARD

This colorful reptile can run really fast on its hind legs, allowing it to see far across the land as it chases bugs and other lizards.

WILD TURKEY

The ancients domesticated both dogs and turkeys. You can still see these large, delicious game birds pecking the ground for nuts.

PITHOUSES

Before the Ancestral Pueblo people built their magnificent palaces, they lived in pithouses on the top of the mesa and sometimes in the alcoves, where they later built towers. These pithouses were partly underground, supported by timbers, and topped with a roof made of branches and clay. They usually featured two rooms: an antechamber likely used for storage and a main room with a fire and a smoke hole.

PINYON JAY

The dusky blue pinyon jay stores thousands of seeds each year, mostly from pine trees. Thanks to an excellent memory, it can remember where almost all of them are.

MIDDEN

A midden is basically a fancy word for a heap of trash. Just outside of their homes, the Ancestral Pueblo people tossed their garbage—broken pots, corncobs, old tools, leftover dinner scraps. Now these middens are treasure troves for archaeologists, who sift through the sand to find clues to the ancients' way of life. In both middens and dwellings, archaeologists have discovered artifacts from all over, such as shell necklaces from the coast, copper bells from Mexico, and macaw feathers from Central America.

PINYON MOUSE
Mostly nocturnal, this mouse dwells in the pinyon-juniper woodlands and only lives to about a year of age.

GRAY FOX
Thanks to a rotating forearm, gray foxes are the only canine species that climb trees. Sometimes they'll even den in a hollow trunk.

TURKEY VULTURE
These scavengers soar on six-foot wingspans and follow their noses to their favorite food: smelly dead animals!

MANO AND METATE
Centuries ago, women used a grinding stone (mano) and surface (metate) to pound corn before cooking it. Corn was grown in Mesa Verde as early as AD 450.

KIVA

Kivas were basically the synagogues, mosques, or churches of today. The ancients used handmade ladders to descend into these round underground chambers to perform ceremonies and take shelter.

PINYON PINE
This hardy tree may only start reproducing around 50 years of age. The Ancestral Puebloans relied on pine nuts for protein. They also used the wood for house posts and fires.

GLACIER

Scientists believe these glaciers are at least 7,000 years old. Over time, they've carved the land into beautiful valleys, rocky horns, and fins as sharp as a dolphin's.

YELLOWSTONE

Bears, wolves, bison, and elk are just a few of the critters you can see in America's first national park, founded for its gushing geysers and canyon scenery.

GRAND TETON

These dark, spiky mountains are so steep that rock climbers scale them with harnesses, ropes, and rubber-coated shoes. There's no room for error!

ROCKY MOUNTAINS

That high-pitched whistle and roar is the sound of an elk bugling to attract a mate in this park full of forests, alpine meadows, and stony peaks.

GREAT SAND DUNES

What's the best way to get from the top to the bottom of a massive sand dune? On a sled, of course!

ROCKY MOUNTAINS

BLACK CANYON OF THE GUNNISON

Peer over the edge of this steep, dark canyon to see cliffs that drop as far as 2,700 feet into the earth. Rock climbers scale these intimidating walls.

Rising more than 14,000 feet into the western sky, the great Rocky Mountains stretch clear from Canada to Mexico. This wall of peaks posed quite an obstacle to America's early fur traders, adventurers, and pioneers. Roads now traverse the range, but it's still rugged travel. Hike up steep mountains to see the same animals that were here centuries ago: packs of wolves, mountain goats, grizzly bears, wolverines, and elk. Explore massive white glaciers, climb up the tallest sand dunes in North America, and listen to the deafening roar of waterfalls. This is a place for adventure, whether it's skiing down slopes or whitewater rafting a rowdy river!

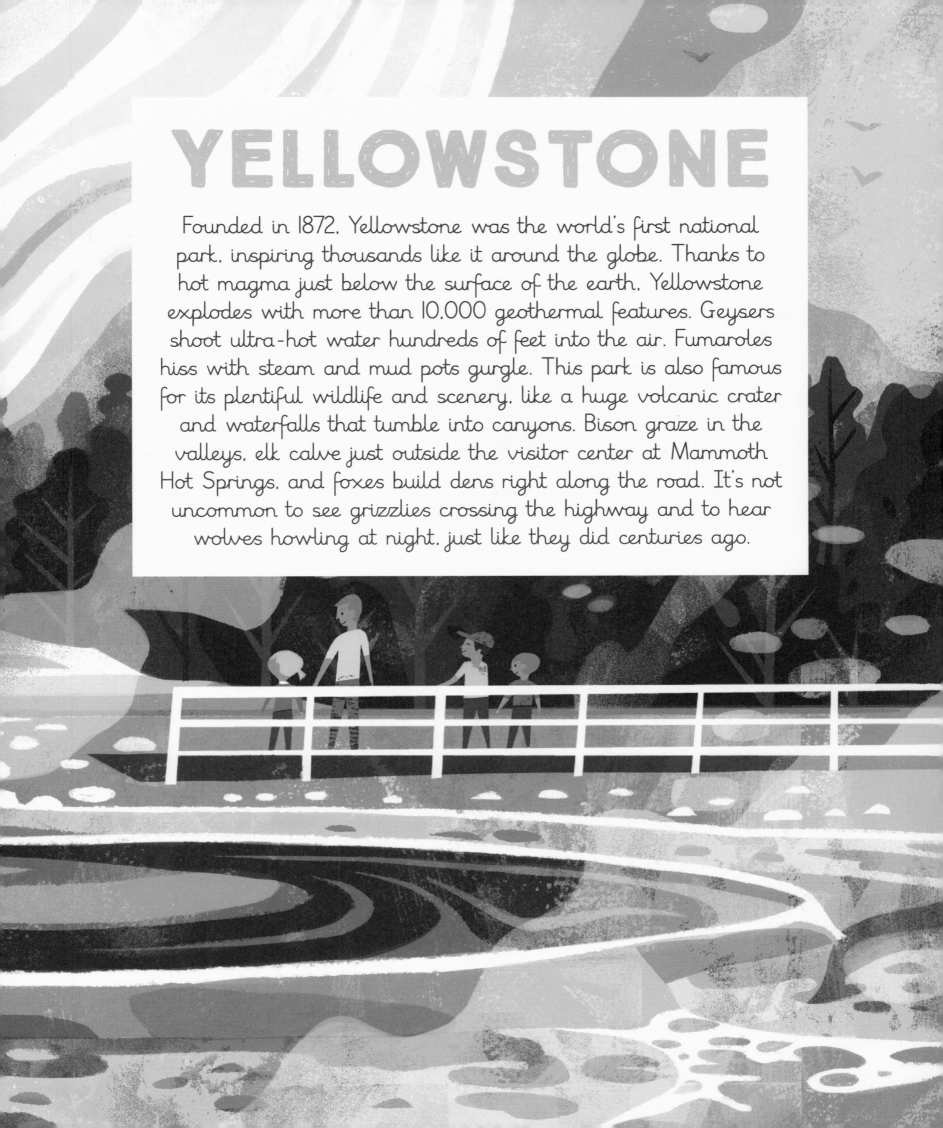

YELLOWSTONE

Founded in 1872, Yellowstone was the world's first national park, inspiring thousands like it around the globe. Thanks to hot magma just below the surface of the earth, Yellowstone explodes with more than 10,000 geothermal features. Geysers shoot ultra-hot water hundreds of feet into the air. Fumaroles hiss with steam and mud pots gurgle. This park is also famous for its plentiful wildlife and scenery, like a huge volcanic crater and waterfalls that tumble into canyons. Bison graze in the valleys, elk calve just outside the visitor center at Mammoth Hot Springs, and foxes build dens right along the road. It's not uncommon to see grizzlies crossing the highway and to hear wolves howling at night, just like they did centuries ago.

YELLOWSTONE

STATE:
Wyoming, Montana, and Idaho

FOUNDED:
1872

SIZE:
2,221,724 acres

YELLOWSTONE SAND VERBENA
Botanists think this species survives the cold with the help of warm sand from thermal features.

GRIZZLY BEAR
Grizzly bears weigh up to 700 pounds and have huge curved claws, but they are mostly vegetarian.

WARM SPRINGS SPIKE-RUSH
This green plant grows in mats only in waters around 80 degrees— temperatures that would kill most flora.

• COLORFUL HOT SPRINGS

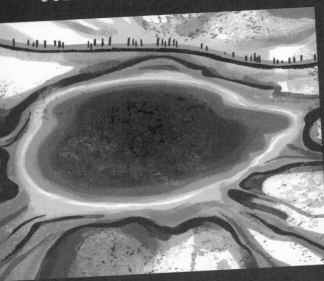

The hot magma under Yellowstone heats up underground water, which then bubbles to the surface, forming hot springs. Many turn crazy colors, like Grand Prismatic Spring. It's not the water that's colored, though. It's tiny bacteria, known as thermophiles, which can withstand some of the hottest, most acidic waters on Earth.

SANDHILL CRANE
These four-foot-tall birds gather in flocks in marshes and grasslands in summer. When mating, they spread their wings, call, and jump in a spectacular dance.

LODGEPOLE PINE
Native Americans used this long, straight pine to make their lodges and tipis. With shallow roots, lodgepoles can keel over in windstorms.

ELK

As many as 20,000 elk roam Yellowstone. During the fall mating season, listen for bugling—a long moan and series of impressive screams.

LYNX

These wild cats with tufted ears are so secretive, they've only been spotted 112 times in the history of the park. Do you think you could find one?

GEYSERS

Yellowstone has more geysers than any other place on the planet. Old Faithful is the most famous, erupting in a spectacular 130-foot-tall fountain every 60-110 minutes. But there are lots of others in fanciful forms and shapes. Some geysers spout in bursts and others in fireworks. Some shoot up every few hours, while others only appear every few decades. One, named Steamboat, rockets up to 400 feet in the air, but its eruptions are totally unpredictable!

YELLOWSTONE CUTTHROAT TROUT

Yellowstone River and Yellowstone Lake have the world's largest population of inland cutthroat trout, tasty fish that feed bears, otters, mink, and about 20 species of birds.

AMERICAN DIPPER

The only true aquatic songbird in the country, the dipper has a gland that produces special oil to keep its feathers water-resistant. It spends its time dipping and diving in water for insects.

FOREST FIRES

Fire is a natural and important part of Yellowstone. Every summer, lightning starts dozens of fires, most of which peter out after torching less than half an acre. After fire sweeps through, dead and decaying vegetation is broken down and the soil is enriched by minerals from the ash and sunlight. Around charred trees, a bright carpet of greenery emerges, creating new homes for birds, insects, and other animals.

GLACIER

Glaciers look like massive stationary blocks of ice, but they're actually rivers of frozen water that flow down mountains like conveyor belts. As they move, they grind the landscape into the jagged scenery that you see today. Look for signs of them, such as arêtes: steep sawlike fins carved by two glaciers rubbing a mountain. Skid down moraines, or dip your toes into 40-degree turquoise lakes fed by snowmelt.

This national park is also known for having all of the same animals that were here when the land was the sole territory of indigenous people: bears, wolves, wolverines, bald eagles, and marmots, to name just a few. To see the park's smallest citizens, venture into a stream and turn over a rock to see the creepy crawlies that thrive in the clean mountain water.

GLACIER

STATE:
Montana

FOUNDED:
1910

SIZE:
1,013,379 acres

GLACIERS

Glaciers form when winter snowfall outpaces summer melting. Because of climate change, the glaciers in the national park are receding, and scientists predict they will disappear by 2030. But their marks will remain across the landscape. Look for U-shaped valleys with flat bottoms and steep sides, mountains shaped like horns, and cirques, which are valleys that look like ice cream scoops.

PTARMIGAN
These ground-dwelling birds survive the cold with the help of nostril feathers that warm the air they breathe. Their feathered feet act like snowshoes.

GLACIER LILY
Glacier lilies sprout with six spectacular yellow petals just after the snow melts. Some Native American tribes used to dig up the bulbs for food.

WOLVERINE
This scrappy, ferocious predator weighs only 20-30 pounds but can take down animals as big as elk and chew its way out of traps.

ARMY CUTWORM MOTH
Army cutworm moths grow up on the Great Plains, then fly to the mountains in summer and hide in rock fields. Grizzly bears turn over rocks and eat thousands of them each day.

WHITEBARK PINE
The whitebark pine can withstand high winds, terrible cold, and poor soil, which is why you'll see it high on mountains where no other trees would dare grow.

● TRIPLE DIVIDE PEAK

On top of the Continental Divide, a drop of water can go west and eventually end up in the Pacific Ocean or east to the Atlantic. From the top of Triple Divide Peak, that drop could split in three ways and end up in vastly different places: the Atlantic, Pacific, or the Hudson Bay way up north in Canada. Only two other peaks in the world boast a rare triple drainage system such as this.

MOUNTAIN GOAT

Mountain goats survive 100-mile-per-hour winds and temperatures as low as -50 degrees with the help of their thick two-layered wool coats.

HUCKLEBERRY

Black and brown bears love these purplish blue berries. They're a delicious snack for us too!

HARLEQUIN DUCK

Harlequin ducks like rough water so much that many adults have broken bones from the turbulence. Look for them swimming in rushing rivers and near rapids and waterfalls.

PIKA

A pika is so small it could fit in the palm of your hand. One of the only animals that can survive winter above the tree line, these mammals hide out in talus slopes but don't hibernate.

PATERNOSTER LAKES

Among the many cool features left behind by the glaciers, paternoster lakes form after the hulking ice digs out a string of little bowls on its way down the mountain. They're often linked by a stream and look like the beads on a rosary, which is why they're named paternoster, after the Lord's Prayer.

OLYMPIC

Covering much of Washington's Olympic Peninsula, this park has rugged beaches, dripping rain forests, and mountains that are snow-capped well into the summer.

NORTH CASCADES

These mountains are incredibly steep, rising from cool, old-growth forests to meadows freckled with wildflowers. Farther up, more than 300 glaciers cling to rocky peaks.

CRATER LAKE

About 7,700 years ago, a huge peak collapsed thanks to a big volcanic eruption. Now filled with water, the crater is the deepest lake in America and glows a brilliant shade of blue.

MOUNT RAINIER

An active volcano, Mount Rainier towers 14,410 feet over Washington, as tall as ten Empire State Buildings. It's so high it gets an average of 54 feet of snow every winter.

REDWOOD

More than 300 feet tall, cool redwood forests feel ancient, mysterious and primeval. Relatives of these trees lived during the time of the dinosaurs 160 million years ago.

LASSEN VOLCANIC

Volcanoes and their features are this park's claim to fame. Visit boiling lakes, steaming vents, and Fart Gulch, named for its stinky sulfur, which smells like rotten eggs!

PINNACLES

Rocky spires and talus caves are a few of the wonders you'll see in this 30-mile-wide volcanic field, where volcanoes erupted 23 million years ago.

YOSEMITE

Yosemite is known for its humongous granite monoliths, some of the longest waterfalls in the world, and alpine meadows full of wildflowers and deer.

CHANNEL ISLANDS

These five rocky isles are home to rare animals like the island fox and blue island scrub-jay. The surrounding waters teem with orange fish, seals, and whales.

SEQUOIA & KINGS CANYON

Sequoias, the biggest trees on earth, are whole cities unto themselves. Their canopies are home to all sorts of animals, insects, and plants.

WEST

Feel small as an ant as you explore the majestic open spaces or walk beneath the towering trees, mountains, and volcanoes of the American West, where the national park idea was born. In the Sierra Nevada, giant hunks of granite shoot up into the sky and canyons plunge into the earth. In groves of the world's biggest and tallest trees, sunbeams filter down through the canopies as they would in a beautiful temple. Volcanoes tower over the land, some still steaming—and no one knows exactly when they'll erupt again! While the parks are full of big-league splendor, they also have tiny charms too. Be still and quiet as a hawk to spot shy wildlife from trout to bobcats. Listen to the sounds of nature, from bees buzzing in high mountain meadows to wind rushing over bare pinnacles to waves crashing on magnificent Pacific shores.

YOSEMITE

Lie down in a grassy meadow in Yosemite Valley and look up. Solid granite rocks rise more than a half mile into the sky and waterfalls thunder down their faces for thousands of feet. If you get close, they're so loud you have to shout! Peering through binoculars, you look closely at the cliffs. Those tiny colored dots are rock climbers, who use rubbery shoes to climb the faces and camp a thousand feet up hanging from a tent secured to the rock. On the valley floor, mule deer graze, squirrels forage for acorns, and skunks scurry about the underbrush. (If one does a headstand, you know he's ready to spray.) When you crawl into your own tent at night, make sure you don't leave food or trash out—black bears are common and love to steal snacks!

YOSEMITE

STATE:
California

FOUNDED:
1980

SIZE:
748,436 acres

YOSEMITE CAVE PSEUDOSCORPION
Scientists only discovered this tiny scorpion-like insect in 2010. It is blind, the size of a fingernail, and only known to live in two caves.

FISHER
These furry predators are a little bigger than house cats but much more ferocious. They are one of the few species that can kill a porcupine without looking like a pincushion.

MULE DEER
These deer are named after mules because of their enormous ears, which rotate toward you when you catch their attention.

MEADOWS

Yosemite has more than 3,000 meadows that attract crowds of wildlife. In summer, milkweed blooms and monarchs brighten the grass with their orange and black wings. Deer graze, dragonflies zoom about, and red-winged blackbirds fill the air with song. If you're lucky and have keen eyes, you might even spot a bobcat stalking the grass for small prey. Meadows are important places for us too. Yosemite's meadows filter water that supplies most of San Francisco.

ACORN WOODPECKER
Acorn woodpeckers drill as many as 50,000 holes into a single tree, then store acorns inside of them for winter.

• BLACK OAK

Black oak acorns are the most delicious of all of California's acorns and were prized sources of protein and fat for Native Americans. They used to set small fires under the oaks to clear out underbrush and create good conditions for them to grow.

BOBCAT

Bobcats live all over, from deserts to the Everglades, but they're rarely seen because of their secretive nature. Identify one by its tufted ears and short, black-tipped tail.

INCENSE CEDAR

In poor conditions, incense cedars sometimes grow as little as three feet in three decades. Good thing they can live for 500 years.

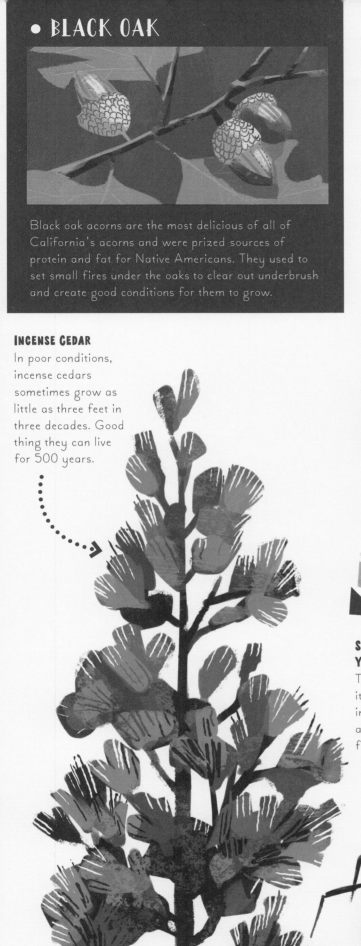

SCARLET MONKEYFLOWER

The brilliant red blooms of the monkeyflower attract hummingbirds, which carry pollen to other flowers and help them reproduce.

SIERRA NEVADA YELLOW-LEGGED FROG

This endangered amphibian uses its long sticky tongue to catch insects and slurp them up. They also occasionally eat tadpoles, dead frogs, and even their own eggs!

WATERFALLS

As the snow melts in spring, Yosemite comes alive with the sounds of rushing water. Yosemite Falls is the largest waterfall in the park and fifth biggest in the world, tumbling 2,425 feet. In winter, the waterfalls slow down, but on cold mornings their spray creates sparkling white frames of frost. At night, look for rare moonbows, rainbows formed by the light of the full moon that appear in the waterfalls' mist.

BLACK WIDOW SPIDER

Female black widows have shiny bodies with the telltale red hourglass on their bellies. They are highly venomous but only strike when provoked.

71

OLYMPIC

Zip up your raincoat! You're in a deep, dark, silent rain forest that smells of cedar. More than 12 feet of rain drench this forest each year, which is why the ground feels like a sponge under your feet. Bright orange mushrooms polka-dot the ground and ferns and mosses carpet every surface. This national park also has two other wildly different landscapes. On the coast, wade into a tide pool to see what you can find—anemones, mussels, sea stars, and crabs. One visitor found a fossilized sea star between 5 and 24 million years old! Within miles of shore, the mountains rise more than 7,000 feet. Walk through meadows with wildflowers taller than you as marmots and chipmunks dart into holes. So much snow falls here that you can still go sledding in July!

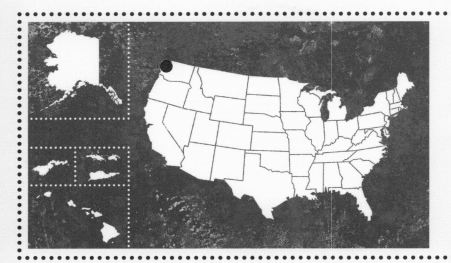

OLYMPIC

STATE:
Washington

FOUNDED:
1938

SIZE:
922,691 acres

FIDDLEHEAD FERN
Look closely at the forest floor for the tiny spirals of baby ferns. Known as fiddleheads, they are a delicious springtime delicacy.

OLYMPIC MARMOT
Listen for sharp whistles as you hike in a high mountain meadow—that's the sound of an Olympic marmot, a playful, roly-poly cat-sized rodent.

AVALANCHES

When rocks or soil come loose and tumble down slopes, they're called rockslides or mudslides. When snow comes loose, it's an avalanche. Avalanches typically happen on steep, open slopes after a storm when the new snow hasn't bonded to the old snow. Within about five seconds of letting loose, an avalanche can reach 80 miles per hour, sound as loud as a jet, and emit a huge cloud of snow.

ORCA/KILLER WHALE
Each pod of orcas speaks its own language of screams, whistles, and clicks. These dialects are passed down through the generations.

BANANA SLUG
Watch your step . . . bright yellow banana slugs cross trails on tracks of their own slime. These mollusks are hermaphrodites. Each one is both male and female, but slugs rarely mate with themselves.

SITKA SPRUCE
This evergreen tree likes the cool, humid weather of the Pacific Northwest coast. Its wood has been used for everything from musical instruments to World War II airplanes.

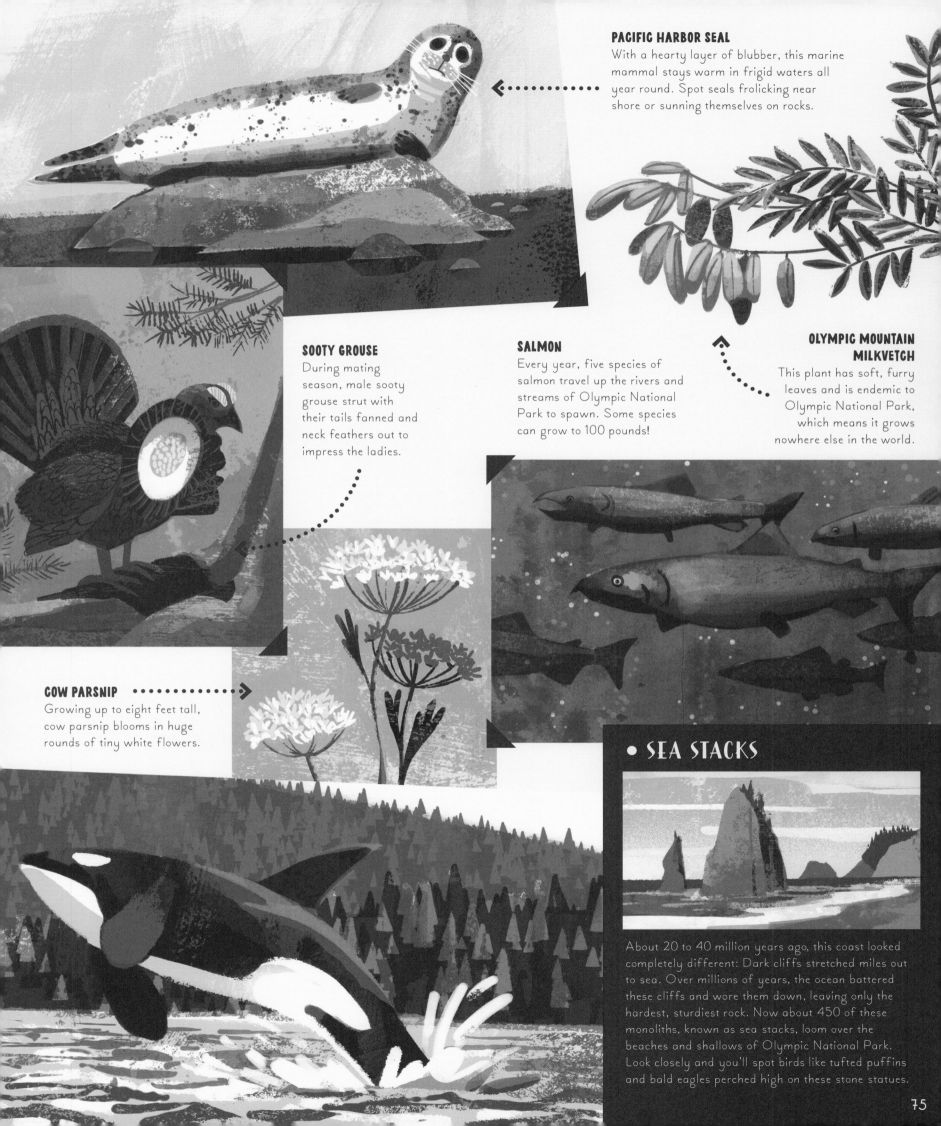

PACIFIC HARBOR SEAL

With a hearty layer of blubber, this marine mammal stays warm in frigid waters all year round. Spot seals frolicking near shore or sunning themselves on rocks.

SOOTY GROUSE

During mating season, male sooty grouse strut with their tails fanned and neck feathers out to impress the ladies.

SALMON

Every year, five species of salmon travel up the rivers and streams of Olympic National Park to spawn. Some species can grow to 100 pounds!

OLYMPIC MOUNTAIN MILKVETCH

This plant has soft, furry leaves and is endemic to Olympic National Park, which means it grows nowhere else in the world.

COW PARSNIP

Growing up to eight feet tall, cow parsnip blooms in huge rounds of tiny white flowers.

• SEA STACKS

About 20 to 40 million years ago, this coast looked completely different: Dark cliffs stretched miles out to sea. Over millions of years, the ocean battered these cliffs and wore them down, leaving only the hardest, sturdiest rock. Now about 450 of these monoliths, known as sea stacks, loom over the beaches and shallows of Olympic National Park. Look closely and you'll spot birds like tufted puffins and bald eagles perched high on these stone statues.

CHANNEL ISLANDS

You're paddling a kayak off Santa Cruz Island when a seal pokes her head out of the water just off your bow and eyes you playfully. Beneath your boat, kelp forests sway and bright orange garibaldi damselfish dart right below the surface. These waters are chock full of creatures—and so are these craggy isles. The Channel Islands are only 10 to 60 miles from Los Angeles. But since they have never been connected to the mainland, they harbor almost 150 species of plants and animals that live nowhere else in the world. Hike through the hills to spot a blue island scrub-jay or a small island fox— one of the rarest foxes on earth— slinking through the grass.

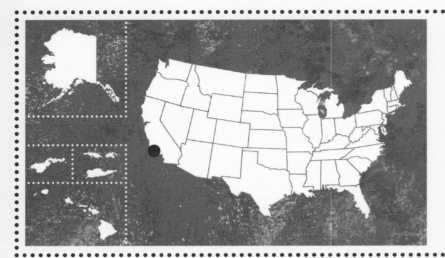

CHANNEL ISLANDS

STATE:
California

FOUNDED:
1980

SIZE:
249,576 acres

GIANT KELP
Giant kelp sprouts in waters up to 100 feet deep and grows as fast as two feet per day. These underwater forests shelter more than 1,000 different species of animals and plants.

SUNFLOWER STAR
The sunflower star grows up to 24 arms and comes in zany colors—pink, purple, yellow, orange, green, and brown. Its bones are disconnected so it can open its mouth really wide and swallow animals whole.

ISLAND OAK
Native Americans used to collect the acorns of this rare oak. They boiled the tannin out of them, smashed it up, and ate it.

GIANT BLACK SEA BASS
At the bottom of the kelp forests, giant sea bass grow way bigger than we do—up to seven feet long and 800 pounds!

• PRESIDENT OBAMA'S LICHEN

The northern Channel Islands host about 400 lichen species, the most diverse collection in the whole state. In late 2007, a researcher found a new species of lichen and named it after the newly elected president to honor him for his support of scientific research.

ISLAND SCRUB-JAY
A relative of the raven, the brilliant blue scrub-jay only lives on Santa Cruz Island, which means it has the smallest range of any bird on the continent.

GIANT COREOPSIS
This unusual plant grows up to six feet tall and sprouts dozens of beautiful yellow, daisy-like flowers from its giant woody stalks.

FOSSILIZED PYGMY MAMMOTH

In 1994, on Santa Rosa Island, paleontologists unearthed a rare find: the most complete fossilized pygmy mammoth in the world. Compared to mammoths, which grew about 14 feet tall, pygmy mammoths were shrimps—just 4.5 to 7 feet tall. But their small size allowed them to get by with less food, which helped them survive on these islands.

ISLAND FOX
The island fox, which only lives here, was almost extinct in the 1990s. Thanks to scientists who bred foxes in captivity and vaccinated wild ones, there are now more than 3,000 in the park—the fastest recovery of an endangered species.

NORTHERN ELEPHANT SEAL
The second largest seals in the world, elephant seals can dive deeper than 5,000 feet and hold their breath for an hour and a half. How long can you hold your breath?

GREAT WHITE SHARK
Weighing as much as 7,300 pounds, the great white shark is one of the ocean's most feared meat eaters, but they rarely attack humans.

SEQUOIA & KINGS CANYON

Look up! You're standing in a grove of giant sequoias, the biggest trees in the world. The very largest, the General Sherman Tree, is taller than a 27-story building and wider than a three-lane highway. This behemoth plant is home to tons of other living beings. Little brown bats roost in sequoias' foliage and under loose bark. The northern flying squirrel glides between branches on thin wings, and worms, snails, scorpions, spiders, and flowers all live and grow in the tree. Next door, Sequoia's sister park, Kings Canyon, is also known for really big things. Large black bears roam the forests. Mount Whitney, the tallest peak in the continental United States, rises to 14,494 feet, and Kings Canyon plummets more than a mile and a half into the earth!

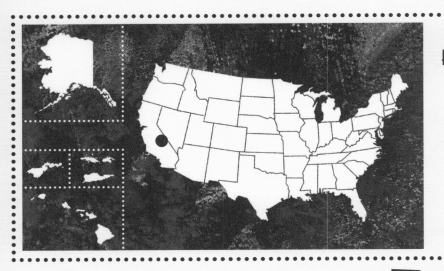

SEQUOIA AND KINGS CANYON

STATE:
California

FOUNDED:
1890 & 1940

SIZE:
865,964
total acres

POISON OAK
Watch out for this common poison ivy relative, which has groups of three lobed leaves. The oil in this plant causes a very itchy rash.

TOWNSEND'S BIG-EARED BAT
In winter, these funny-looking bats hibernate in caves, sometimes in groups of more than 1,000. Moths are their favorite food.

LEOPARD LILY
Native Americans dig up leopard lily bulbs to eat. Find this striking flower near streams and in low soggy meadows.

SOUTHERN FOXTAIL PINE
Only found in California, the southern foxtail pine grows very slowly on high, harsh, cold mountaintops. Its thick bark protects it from forest fires.

CALIFORNIA QUAIL
Find this quail in brushy areas at low elevations. Offspring leave the nest the day after hatching and can already find their own food!

GRANITE
Most of the peaks and canyons in these parks are made of granitic stone, which forms when molten rock cools far below the earth's surface. Now those rocks form huge gray bowls and the tall peaks of the Sierra Nevada. It's a relatively young mountain range that scientists believe is less than 40 million years old. In fact, the mountains are still growing today. With every earthquake, they gain a little height!

● WILDERNESS

As more land is crowded with human beings, plants and animals need refuges where they can grow without our interference. In 1964, the United States became the first country to set aside wilderness areas where nature could thrive untrammeled by people. About 97% of Sequoia and Kings Canyon National Parks are wilderness, which means there are no roads, buildings, or signs of humans other than trails. In these wild areas, you can walk for days without seeing another person and experience nature in its raw state.

SACRAMENTO SUCKER
Sacramento suckers are found in the calm pools of streams and have big, fleshy lips.

CALIFORNIA KINGSNAKE
Visitors commonly spot California kingsnakes at low elevations. Look for a dark brown or black body with white stripes.

GIANT SEQUOIA TREE
These woody giants have tannin, an acidic substance, in their bark. It's like a superpower, protecting them from fires, rot, and insects. As a result, they can live for more than 3,000 years.

MONARCH BUTTERFLY
Monarchs are the only known butterflies to migrate two ways like birds. Some fly more than 3,000 miles to reach warmer weather.

SIERRA NEVADA BIGHORN SHEEP
Bighorn sheep are expert climbers, leaping from rock to rock without falling. They give birth way above the tree line—around 12- or 13,000 feet—to avoid predators.

GATES OF THE ARCTIC

The Arctic is an extreme landscape of peaks, rivers bigger than interstate highways, and some of the greatest caribou herds on earth. The Inupiat people still live off this harsh land.

KOBUK VALLEY

About 14,000 years ago, receding glaciers ground rocks into sand, creating massive golden dunes. With summer temperatures reaching 100 degrees, this place can feel like the Sahara!

LAKE CLARK

Lake Clark protects a magnificent salmon run. Every year, more than 300,000 sockeye salmon travel from the ocean to the rivers to spawn. Bears, wolves, and humans survive off of them.

KATMAI

In 1912, a volcano shot ash 100,000 feet into the sky, collapsed Mount Katmai and created the Valley of Ten Thousand Smokes. Now thousands of vents let out curling tendrils of steam.

KENAI FJORDS

The Harding Icefield is thousands of feet thick and feeds nearly 40 glaciers, which have sculpted this landscape into steep, water-filled valleys known as fjords.

ALASKA

DENALI

Mountaineers come from around the world to climb the highest peak in North America, the fearsome Denali. Far below, grizzlies and Dall sheep wander the alpine tundra, forests, and cliffs.

WRANGELL-ST. ELIAS

America's biggest national park is larger than Switzerland. Discover glaciers, volcanoes, mountains and plenty of bears in this vast wilderness.

Just about everything in the 49th state is bigger and gnarlier than in the Lower 48. The peaks are higher and the winters colder. The rivers are wider and the animals scarier. Naturally, that's what people come here for: a big adventure!

Some parks in this state don't even have trails—hikers just set out into the backcountry to hike over tundra, cross thundering rivers, and bushwhack through willows. Others grab ice axes and crampons to climb mountains that rise past the clouds or jump on a boat to watch the whales. Glaciers are everywhere, engraving the land with beautiful valleys and filling pools with ice-cold water. Winters are dark and cold but the aurora borealis decorates the sky with glowing colors. Come summer, in the far north, the sun never disappears below the horizon and it's daylight for 24 hours, a phenomenon called the midnight sun.

GLACIER BAY

Craaaaaaack! That's the sound of a glacier calving icebergs in Glacier Bay, where whales, seals, and sea otters frolic in the cold, deep waters.

Denali

The air is thin and it's -10 degrees as you plod up a snowy mountain with your down suit, goggles, boots, and crampons. This is the tallest peak on the continent, the 20,310-foot Denali. You're so high you can see the curve of the earth on the horizon. Far below, the rest of this park is a vast wilderness of wind-battered peaks, boreal forests, tundra, and braided rivers. This place is BIG and so is the wildlife. Half-ton grizzly bears lumber about looking for berries and roots. Wolf packs sneak up on caribou herds as they graze. And see those white dots on the cliffs? Those are Dall sheep in their very steep homes.

DENALI

STATE:
Alaska

FOUNDED:
1917

SIZE:
6,075,030 acres

SNOWSHOE HARE
In autumn, the snowshoe hare molts its brown-and-gray coat in order to grow a white one that blends in perfectly with the snow.

CARIBOU
It's tough to be a caribou calf. More than half of Denali's calves don't make it past the first two weeks of life because wolves, moose, coyotes, and even golden eagles eat them.

BLACK SPRUCE
This evergreen grows in harsh conditions and acidic soil just above the permafrost, another name for permanently frozen soil. Even a tiny, stunted spruce could be more than 100 years old.

SLED DOGS

So much snow falls in Denali National Park that the roads close every winter. So how do rangers patrol the wilderness? On dogsleds! These Alaskan huskies are the only sled dogs in the country that help protect a national park. Alaska Natives have been using this mode of transportation for thousands of years. Today these dogs are still more reliable than snowmobiles. Even in temperatures of -40, all they need is some food and off they go!

MARSH LABRADOR TEA
Labrador tea seeds know to sprout when the soil gets warm and the days grow long. There's almost 24 hours of daylight here in summer!

WOOD FROG
This fingernail-sized amphibian stops its heart, turns to ice, and appears dead all winter. In spring, within hours of thawing, it's hopping around again.

DINOSAUR TRACKS & FOSSILS

About 70 million years ago, a very different cast of wildlife roamed Denali: dinosaurs! Paleontologists have found more than 270 fossil and dinosaur track sites here. Back in the Cretaceous period, the climate was more like the Pacific Northwest's. Imagine metasequoia trees towering over lush ferns and wetlands. Duck-billed dinosaurs as big as school buses stomped around in herds, and predators the size of microwaves soared overhead on 25-foot wingspans.

QUAKING ASPEN

Aspens look like individual trees, but they're actually one big organism connected underground. Each trunk is an identical clone.

DALL SHEEP

Sheep horns grow throughout the year but slow down in late fall during mating season. By counting the rings on horns—called annuli—you can figure out the animal's age.

ARCTIC TERN

Arctic terns are believed to migrate farther than any other bird on the planet—more than 37,000 miles round trip from Antarctica to the Arctic.

• NORTHERN LIGHTS

On a dark night, look up to see curtains of otherworldly green light swirl and flicker across the sky. These are the northern lights, the planet's most spectacular natural light show. Also called the aurora, the phenomenon only occurs in high latitudes when energetic particles from the sun collide with gases in our atmosphere. People travel thousands of miles for a chance to see these eerie multicolored lights.

WOLF

Have you ever heard the sound of a wolf howling? No one knows exactly what the wolves are saying. Perhaps they're trying to find each other or sound the alarm that a rival pack is nearby.

Glacier Bay

About 250 years ago, during a cold period known as the Little Ice Age, Alaska's Grand Pacific Glacier suddenly steamrolled 100 miles down a bay, scouring it of any life and chasing away the Huna Tlingit people who lived here for centuries. Within decades, it reversed its path and receded to the size it is today: 35 miles long and two miles wide. Over the years, plants and animals returned. Walk through quiet rain forests covered in moss. Nearby, grizzly bears waddle, and wolves patrol beaches. From a boat in Glacier Bay, listen for the whoomph of glaciers calving icebergs and the sound of a whale exhaling or crashing into the water in an impressive breach.

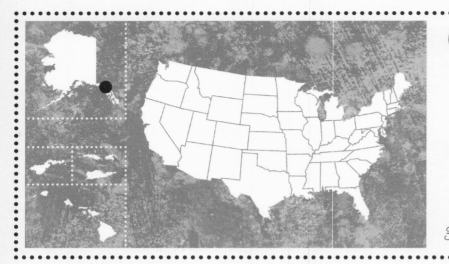

GLACIER BAY

STATE:
Alaska

FOUNDED:
1980

SIZE:
3,280,198 acres

BERRIES

Glacier Bay's forests are teeming with colorful and delicious berries. The Huna Tlingit preserved these tasty treats in thick, smelly seal oil so they'd have plenty to eat during the long winters.

HUNA TRIBAL HOUSE

After the Huna Tlingit were chased out of Glacier Bay by the Grand Pacific Glacier, they established a new village about 30 miles away. Just as they were ready to return to their homeland, the national park was founded. Rangers discouraged them from practicing their traditions, even though this was originally their land. There were a lot of hard feelings, but over the years, the Park Service and the Huna Tlingit developed a friendship. As a sign of peace, the Huna Tlingit constructed a tribal house in the park, the first built there in centuries. Now you can visit the house, which hosts ceremonies, smells deeply of cedar, and is covered in carvings that illustrate Huna stories.

MOUNTAIN GOAT

Find mountain goats hopping along steep rocky bare cliffs. Their hair is hollow to help insulate them from the extreme cold of Glacier Bay winters.

BALD EAGLE

In the 1960s, bald eagles were in danger of going extinct. The U.S. government protected their habitat and banned the pesticide DDT, which damaged their eggs. Now their populations are thriving. Look in the trees near shore to spot their telltale white heads.

PACIFIC HALIBUT

As a halibut grows, one of his eyes moves to the other side of his head so he can lie flat on the ocean floor and still see everything passing by.

DEVIL'S CLUB

Devil's club has enormous leaves and thorny, poisonous stalks. Alaska Natives have used it for everything from a remedy for arthritis to fishhooks and deodorant.

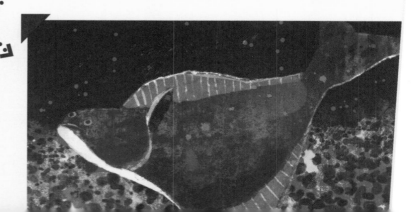

GRIZZLY BEAR

While black bears prefer forests, grizzlies live all over the park, eating everything from berries and plants to salmon and dead animals.

HUMPBACK WHALE

These gentle, endangered giants come to Glacier Bay every summer to gorge themselves on fish. In one gulp, a humpback can take in 15,000 gallons of water—more than your house uses in five months!

TUFTED PUFFIN

Puffins are great swimmers and decent fliers, but it takes them quite some effort to get off the water and into the air.

WESTERN HEMLOCK

You'll see lots of western hemlocks in Glacier Bay's forests because they love the rich, moist soil and the beautiful, swirling fog.

FJORDS

As glaciers advance, they carve sheer, deep valleys. When they're close to the ocean, these valleys fill with seawater and are called fjords. In Glacier Bay, fjords plunge as deep as 1,400 feet and are often dotted with icebergs. The water is very cold and rich in oxygen. These are great conditions for tiny organisms like plankton and things that eat plankton like colorful cold-water corals.

SEA OTTER

In the 19th and 20th centuries, fur traders hunted sea otters almost to extinction. These playful creatures have recovered thanks to an international treaty and other protections. In Glacier Bay, they've boomed from five animals in 1993 to more than 8,000 now.

AMERICAN SAMOA

Deep in the South Pacific Ocean, National Park of American Samoa is a classic island paradise. Imagine white-sand beaches fringed with teal water and jungles where fruit bats hang upside down from the trees.

To get to America's farthest-flung territories, you must travel deep into the oceans. Some of these islands are located thousands of miles from the mainland. In these remote steamy paradises, smell the salty breeze that travels over the ocean and rustles your hair. Float in the warm waters of tropical seas, dive down to explore coral reefs brimming with fish, or survey the debris from slave ships that were wrecked offshore centuries ago. When you return to the surface, marvel at the fiery volcanoes that crafted these lands and continue to shape them today. Indigenous people have lived on some of the islands since long before the U.S. became a country. Much has changed, but many of the native people still collect fish to eat, make traditional and beautiful hand-crafted items, and perform dances and ceremonies like their ancestors did for centuries before them.

TROPICS

VIRGIN ISLANDS

On the Caribbean Island of St. John, hike through humid rain forests and sink into turquoise water to see rays, turtles, and rainbow-hued fish. This park also protects treasures from a deep and varied history.

HALEAKALA

On the island of Maui, the volcano Haleakala rises from sea level to over 10,000 feet, creating very different weather zones. You could be sweating in a soggy rain forest one minute, then shivering in a cinder desert the next!

HAWAII VOLCANOES

On the Big Island of Hawaii, two active volcanoes rumble, spit magma, and flow with red-hot fiery lava. Legend holds that this is the home of the fire goddess Pele.

HAWAII
VOLCANOES

On the Big Island of Hawaii, Kilauea's hot lava lake casts a fiery glow. From the nearby observation deck, watch as it occasionally spatters the mountain with magma as hot as 2,400 degrees! This park protects two of the world's most active volcanoes, Mauna Loa and Kilauea, and the bizarre landscapes they leave behind. Walk through black lands full of weird shapes of hardened lava. Marvel at statue-like lava trees. And hike through the rain forest, entering a deep, dark tube that once oozed molten rock. The landscape seems harsh, but it has hosted humans for centuries. While visiting, keep an eye out for native Hawaiians' homesteads and 23,000 petroglyphs carved into rocks centuries ago.

HAWAII VOLCANOES

STATE:
Hawaii

FOUNDED:
1916

SIZE:
333,086 acres

HAPU'U (HAWAIIAN TREE FERN)
This lush tree fern towers up to 20 feet tall and 15 feet wide, but it grows incredibly slowly—no more than 3.5 inches a year.

NĒNĒ (HAWAIIAN GOOSE)
These endemic geese had a tough couple of centuries. People hunted them and collected their eggs. Mongooses, dogs, and cats ate them. Even golfers have accidentally whacked the geese with golf balls! In 1951, there were only about 30 nēnē left. Now, thanks to efforts to breed them in captivity, about 2,500 live in the wild.

'I'IWI (SCARLET HONEYCREEPER)
With its long beak, the 'i'iwi can slurp up nectar from long, tubular flowers. Its call sounds like a squeaky hinge, just like its name.

'AHINAHINA (MAUNA LOA SILVERSWORD)
These rare plants have swordlike leaves with silvery hairs, and they only grow on Mauna Loa. Between the ages of 10 and 30, the plant shoots a stalk of flowers as high as nine feet tall then abruptly dies.

OPAE'ULA (HAWAIIAN RED POND SHRIMP, ALSO SOMETIMES CALLED VOLCANO SHRIMP)
Seahorses love to eat these tiny red shrimp, which only live in anchialine pools, rare ponds in limestone or volcanic rock that have layers of fresh- and saltwater and tons of rare animals.

'ŌHI'A
'Ōhi'a are the most common trees in Hawaii. They bloom constantly, attracting lots of birds and insects.

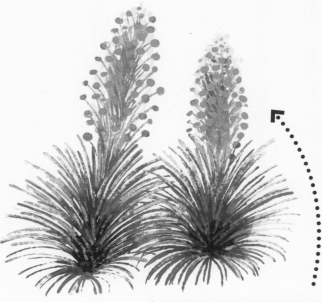

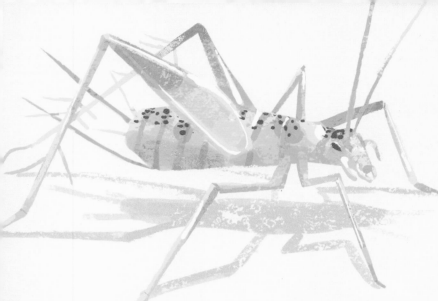

LAVA CRICKET
Hawaiian lava crickets only live on the ceilings of newly formed lava tubes. They eat the roots of plants that burrow down through cracks.

• LAVA TUBES

As hot lava travels downhill, it cuts a channel like a river. When the surface of the stream hits the cool air, it hardens fast, creating a tunnel. Once the flow of lava stops, a long, skinny cave known as a lava tube remains. Inside, there are wild formations that only occur in lava tubes, such as soda straw stalactites that hang from the ceiling in beautiful delicate threads.

HONU'EA (HAWKSBILL SEA TURTLE)
Highly endangered sea turtles come to three beaches in the park to lay eggs. The hatchlings are vulnerable to mongooses, cats, dogs, crabs, and other predators. As few as one in 1,000 make it to adulthood.

'IO (HAWAIIAN HAWK)
The endangered 'io is endemic to Hawaii and only nests on the Big Island. In Hawaiian culture, it is a symbol of royalty.

PELE

According to local culture, Pele, the Hawaiian volcano goddess, lives inside Halema'uma'u, the erupting summit caldera of Kilauea. When you see the red-orange molten lava, you know that she's home. Local Hawaiians frequently come to the park to pay their respects to this important goddess through hula dancing, chanting, and ceremonies.

KOA
During the first five years of life, a koa grows as fast as five feet annually. Its wood is valuable and has been used to make houses, spears, paddles, and even surfboards. In the Hawaiian language, koa means bold, fearless warrior.

VIRGIN
ISLANDS

It's 75 degrees and sunny. Feel the warm sand between your toes and wade into the turquoise waters of the Virgin Islands. Just offshore of St. John, seagrass beds and coral reefs teem with fish as colorful as confetti. Put on your snorkel and watch as a whitespotted filefish changes color before your eyes and a friendly polka-dotted trunkfish poses for your underwater camera. There's even an ancient underwater fish pen probably constructed by the Taino people who lived here centuries ago. On land, explore the spooky stone ruins of sugar plantations built in the 1700s and hike through rain forests that smell like tropical fruit trees. At the top of the hill, you can gaze over the sparkling Caribbean Sea. What would it have been like to see Christopher Columbus's ship on the horizon?

VIRGIN ISLANDS

TERRITORY:
Virgin Islands

FOUNDED:
1956

SIZE:
15,135 acres

PARROTFISH
Every night, certain species of parrotfish create a clear mucus sac to sleep in like pajamas. Scientists believe it masks their scent, keeping them safe from predators.

GOLDEN ORB SPIDER
These black-and-yellow spiders spin beautiful webs made of golden silk. The threads are believed to be stronger than bulletproof vests and have been used to make rare garments.

TROPICAL FRUIT
Virgin Islands National Park's forests are dotted with wild fruit trees that smell fragrant and sweet. In the foliage, look closely for soursop, papaya, mango, sugar apple, and calabash, which can grow to the size of basketballs.

FISHING BAT (OR GREATER BULLDOG BAT)
Echolocation consists of making a sound and listening for its echo to determine an object's location. Fishing bats use the technique to detect ripples in the surface of the water, then nab fish and insects with their long claws.

MORAY EEL
Don't stick your hand into a dark hole in the reef—a sharp-toothed moray eel might live there and mistake your finger for a fish!

PLANTATIONS AND THE SLAVE TRADE

Like many other islands in the Caribbean in the 17th and 18th centuries, Europeans colonized St. John. They whacked down much of the rain forest and planted sugarcane to feed the growing hunger for yummy sweets. Tragically, they brought enslaved people from Africa to work the plantations in terrible conditions. The Dutch abolished slavery in the Virgin Islands in 1848. In 1917, the U.S. bought the islands from Denmark. Today, you can still see the stone ruins of the old sugarcane plantations and mills—and even a dungeon—hidden in the greenery of this national park.

SEA FANS

Sea fans are soft corals, which are actually large colonies of tiny animals. They grow across the current so they can net plankton to eat.

TEYER PALM

The only native palm left in the park, pieces of the Teyer were used for baskets, brooms, fish traps, and roofing by native people.

KAPOK TREE

These common trees produce seed pods packed with silky fibers that are very buoyant. The fibers have been used for life preservers and stuffing for pillows.

GREEN SEA TURTLE

The largest of all the hard-shelled turtles, the green sea turtle grows as big as 350 pounds on a diet of plants and algae.

MAGNIFICENT FRIGATEBIRD

Magnificent frigatebirds nest in colonies, but they better not leave their homes unattended—their neighbors might come by and eat their eggs!

• WINDS

Surrounded by sea, St. John is at the whim of the winds. Blowing east to west, the trade winds blow clear across the Atlantic, sometimes blanketing the island in dust from the Sahara Desert. In the summer and fall, hurricanes rage through, tearing the leaves from trees and strewing branches all over the island. What's the upside of consistent winds? When it's not storming, it's a great place to cruise around in a sailboat!

CAN YOU SPOT THIS A-Z OF WILDLIFE FROM THE NATIONAL PARKS?

A Quaking aspen

B Bison

C Caribou

D Desert tortoise

E Elk

F Gray fox

G Grizzly bear

H Hawksbill sea turtle

I Island fox

J Javelina

K Kangaroo rat

L Loon

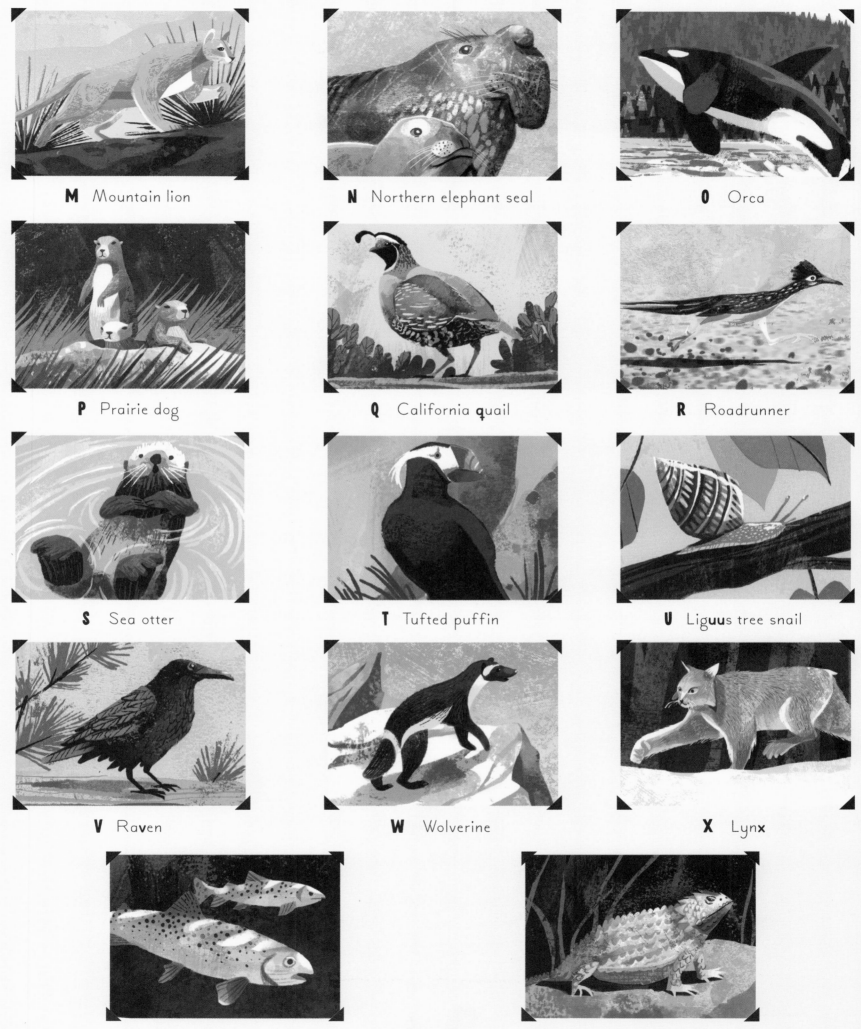

M Mountain lion

N Northern elephant seal

O Orca

P Prairie dog

Q California quail

R Roadrunner

S Sea otter

T Tufted puffin

U Liguus tree snail

V Raven

W Wolverine

X Lynx

Y Yellowstone cutthroat trout

Z Short-horned lizard

YOU CAN HELP PROTECT THE GREAT NATIONAL PARKS

You've come to the end of your journey, and by now you've realized that the national parks are pretty fantastic. But did you know that they're also surprisingly fragile? Their welfare depends on people like you and me who care about and protect them.

The parks haven't always been well cared for. Back in the 19th century, when the national-park idea was new, travelers didn't really know how to behave. Some visitors shot the wildlife, fished out the streams, and even pried off pieces of geyser rock to take home as souvenirs. Some even fed the bears! (That made the creatures connect humans with food. Not such a good idea, right?) Thankfully, the army swooped in, and soldiers protected the animals from poachers. In 1916, the National Park Service was founded to steward these lands.

Today we know it's not cool to feed the animals—of any size—steal artifacts, leave graffiti, or chuck trash into the bushes. There are still threats to parks, such as climate change, air pollution, and dangers like unwise mining and development. But the best thing you can do is to go out and experience the parks, learn about them, love them, and spread the word so that everyone knows how important they are.

Get out of the car and into the mountains, deserts, beaches, and tundra! Drink in new scents and listen to the sounds of creatures, water, and wind. Let the marvels of national parks stoke your curiosity and be sure to bring that zest for exploring home with you. The parks might be grand examples of what nature has to offer, but the beauty of the natural world is never far away. Go out into your own neighborhood and see for yourself. What beautiful treasures might you discover, right under your nose?

INDEX

Inspiring | Educating | Creating | Entertaining

Brimming with creative inspiration, how-to projects, and useful information to enrich your everyday life, Quarto Knows is a favourite destination for those pursuing their interests and passions. Visit our site and dig deeper with our books into your area of interest: Quarto Creates, Quarto Cooks, Quarto Homes, Quarto Lives, Quarto Drives, Quarto Explores, Quarto Gifts, or Quarto Kids.

First Published in 2018 by Wide Eyed Editions, an imprint of The Quarto Group.
400 First Avenue North, Suite 400, Minneapolis, MN 55401, USA.
T (612) 344-8100 F (612) 344-8692 **www.QuartoKnows.com**

A catalogue record for this book is available from the British Library.

ISBN 9781847809766

The illustrations were created digitally
Set in Pistacho and Scholl Hand Cursive

Published by Jenny Broom
Designed by Nicola Price

Manufactured in Dongguan, China TL042018

9 8 7 6 5 4 3 2 1